ISBN 1 85022 142 1

Published by Dyllansow Truran,
Croft Prince, Mount Hawke, Truro,
Cornwall TR4 8EE

Printed by Troutbeck Press, subsidiary of R. Booth Bookbinder Ltd
Antron Hill, Mabe, Penryn, Cornwall TR10 9HH

Designed by Chema Cruz

Photographs of paintings by Simon Cook and Michael Truscott

Another Shade of Blue

Photograph by Richard Wood

John Miller and Michael Truscott in Sicily

Foreword

It should have been just another job. In the winter of 1987 I was to record a radio interview for the BBC with John Miller at Sancreed House, his former home near Land's End, in West Cornwall. The arrangement was to run through some questions, record the interview and leave. Looking back, I now realise that, in a sense, I have never left.

I was welcomed with colour and laughter, conversation and friendship. A professional interview is normally a highly stylised affair; a courtly dance, a fencing exchange, but that day John and I simply talked. He was open, generous and thoughtful. Here was a man who made the questioner ask questions of himself. Long after the tape had run out there was still so much to say and still so much to discuss.

Since then the years have passed - exhibitions opened, birthdays celebrated, conversations explored, books launched - but his friendship has been both rewarding and enriching. The exaltation in the life both around and within him that was so evident in his conversation and his paintings the day we first met has also remained. The beaches, the landscapes, the interiors; all reverberate with colour and celebrate the day. A John Miller painting offers us a window; a view from the room in which we live. The light outside may dazzle our eyes but the artist enables us to realise what lies beyond. It may still be out of our grasp but now we know it is there.

Few events are genuinely life changing. For me meeting John Miller was just that. The dawn is breaking. It is another day.

Tim Hubbard
Writer and BBC Presenter

Dawn Triptych. Oil

A monograph by Emma Burn

In John Miller's latest work there seem to be two streams that flow throughout the collection. Firstly, he wishes to describe the joy that fills us when we stand before a spectacle that strikes us as miraculous. This can be seen in the Brother Sun and Sister Moon paintings where a figure dances before say, an astonishing sunrise. Secondly, he expresses what it's like going right up to the edge of all we understand, standing on the brink of all that mystifies us and looking into the beyond. A distant figure on the shore, a blazing horizon, or a shimmering white beach - in all of these the observer's gaze is lifted up and transported, encouraged to look for something further.

These two streams are part of the same reverence for life that he has always conveyed in his art. But Miller does it without overdoing it - there's no drama, or pathos, or embellishment, and certainly nothing contrived. The images aren't overworked -their ability to communicate what they do lies in the fact that they speak the language of simplicity itself.

Part of the vocabulary that Miller uses is, of course, colour. Hot blue, aqua that sings, purple that hums with energy. Whether it's a view of Venice shrouded in mist, the tussocky Cornish terrain or a luminous Tresco beach, what draws us in initially is the complete pleasure we experience when we gaze at those colours. What holds us is the intensity of what is being said in the image as a whole.

Looking back over Miller's artistic journey one of the threads that binds each phase together is the fact that each canvas seems to glow with a heat of its own. This is partly as a result of a quest to capture a certain kind of light on canvas. That light is both what attracts him to a landscape and what inspires him to describe it to us.

"It is to be found in Cornwall on what are known by the Cornish as *given days*," writes Miller in his autobiographical book "Leave Tomorrow Behind." "I have found it in Venice and the Greek Islands. In Venice and Cornwall there is another light which is more like peering through folds of muslin. This subject has become another of my elusive searches."

That John Miller is a spiritual man will come as no surprise. He has long-held links with the Franciscans and in 1993 he became a Lay Canon of Truro Cathedral. Quite separately from the Church he has a very rich spiritual life, in the sense that it forms a constant awareness in everything that he does. The relevance of this to his art is that he has always wanted to take our line of vision just that little bit further. In the paintings of the early 70s it was through the branches of bare trees, in the 80s when dwelling on landscapes in Venice, Spain, Tuscany and Greece it was through doorways, arches and across water. Always in his paintings of Cornwall we travel across land and into the horizon.

Paraportiani Mykonos

Another aspect of this spirituality is evident in the fact that he will not use his paintings to talk of the dark things. The reason for this he outlines in "Leave Tomorrow Behind." "Towards the end of the war, at an impressionable age, I saw the news films of Belsen," he writes. "Since then I have tried not to act unkindly towards others. I have a strange notion that a thousand tiny unkind acts could easily add up to something as ghastly and inhuman as the concentration camps. I have concluded that, if I am to paint anything at all, it must be a celebration of all that is good and beautiful in this world."

In 1990 Miller shifted the focus of his vision from what he could see outwardly to what he saw inwardly and embarked on his magnificent Interior Landscapes. Gradually over the years he had been dispensing with detail, and with looser brush strokes, had used light and colour to conjure up the essence of a place. For the time being he abandoned all literal references. It was a brave move and in doing so, it was as though part of the painting was suddenly set free.

What pushed him over this artistic edge was his mother's illness. When she was admitted into a nursing home Miller visited her every day, each time noticing her diminishing physical state and feeling a burning need to communicate with her through his painting.

Says Miller: "It no longer mattered that everyone understood the work. It simply had to speak to her. For the last year of her life she was paralysed. She could move her eyes, which remained full of life and intelligence, and her lips. I knew she was fully conscious, although she could no longer speak. Her inner life, beyond the useless body, was growing in stature every day and it was to that part of her life my paintings had to speak. I found that colour and form were all that mattered if I was to communicate at that deeper level of consciousness. I began to simplify the form so that the colour had enough room and was not clogged up."

Ultra-marine over Violet (detail)

The paintings of this transitional period are as brooding as Miller gets. Driving through the countryside to visit his mother he began to see it with greater intensity and depict the Cornish landscape as if in cross-section. Here we see his greatest use of contrast - purple shafts plunge down into an orange earth under a gleaming turquoise sky - surprisingly for him the works are almost angry.

Canticle of St. Francis on Lelant Beach. Oil

"When I was young I painted scenes from the life of St. Francis on my bedroom walls in my parents' house in London. In 1995 I moved from Sancreed House, after thirty-one years there, to a studio on Lelant Beach and a barn inland. The first year at Lelant I filled sketchbooks with everything I saw on the beach and estuary. I drew fishing boats in and out of Hayle Harbour, people walking their dogs, playing on the beach, paddling or swimming, fishing and flying their kites; the very young and the very old. In particular I saw innocent pleasure. The beach became my world, the backdrop to the whole of life. It seemed to encompass all creation. St. Francis wrote his beautiful canticle to creation eight hundred years ago in Assisi. It is, for me, as fresh and relevant as if only just written on Lelant Beach."

But as the painting continued to go through something of a distillation process this anger became an unwanted detail, and like the rest, it fell away. Instead, the Interior Landscapes opened up to a sense of stillness and grace. Single hues took over - blazing reds, oranges, purples, magentas, blues, yellows - and in each painting a solitary figure stood in an archway, facing away from us, looking into the beyond. Sometimes a horizon in the distance heightened the sense that what we were looking at was a state of transition - that the figure was on the threshold of we knew not what, suspended at some immense moment of realisation.

Miller's use of scale reinforced the enormity of his theme; the tiny, flickering figure, the great arch, the horizon. Observers of Miller's career are constantly astounded by his ability to keep on discovering, and pushing the boundaries back. Of all his different phases, in many ways the most recent paintings follow on from the Interior Landscapes. But if it is possible, he has opened them up even more.

Miller's move from Sancreed, where he lived for 31 years, to the Beach House at Lelant played a significant part in this development. Waking each morning to the sun rising over the estuary, glimpsing Godrevy Lighthouse in the distance, seeing a solitary figure poised to fly a kite on the beach, watching a lone fishing boat returning with its catch. The different rhythm of life at the Beach House has added a new dimension.

River Witch. Gouache

Midsummer Sandspur. Oil

"I love watching people on the beach," says Miller. "I think that is really living – when we are fully engaging in the life that is available – that is truthful and good."

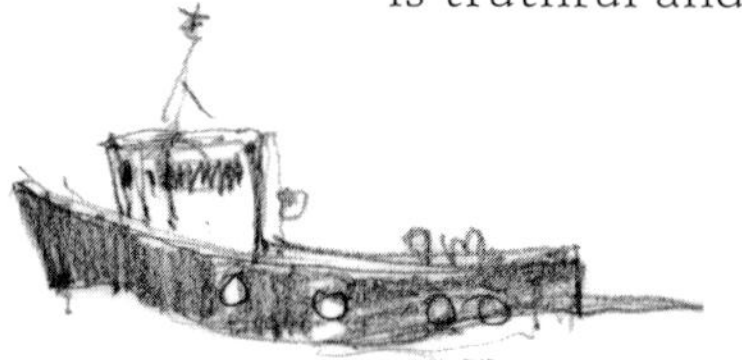

From sketchbooks

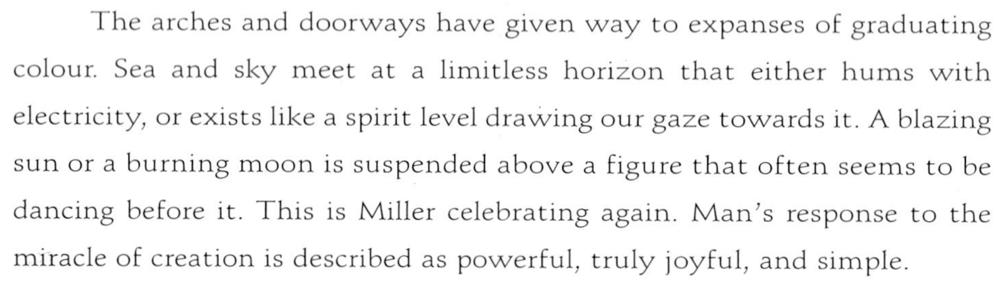

The arches and doorways have given way to expanses of graduating colour. Sea and sky meet at a limitless horizon that either hums with electricity, or exists like a spirit level drawing our gaze towards it. A blazing sun or a burning moon is suspended above a figure that often seems to be dancing before it. This is Miller celebrating again. Man's response to the miracle of creation is described as powerful, truly joyful, and simple.

Beach Figure with Orange Sun. Detail

Again simplicity plays a crucial role in the impact that these images have. The lack of detail takes them on to another level. The paintings are about now, and they're also about forever. But the glowing moment they encompass refuses to get hampered by a particular story. This is what renders Miller's art universal.

Says Miller: "In a funny way the figure in the distance and the solitary boat represent the same thing. When I see an ant scuttling along I'm aware of its life and I'm aware that this is a life that is making its way through time and space and it wants to go on surviving. I think all these paintings are about that. They are part of a tremendous reverence for individual life. Even the sun has a life. I see it growing every morning in this amazing great sky, and as it fulfils its life, it gives life to us, and we do to each other."

Penwith Dawn. Oil

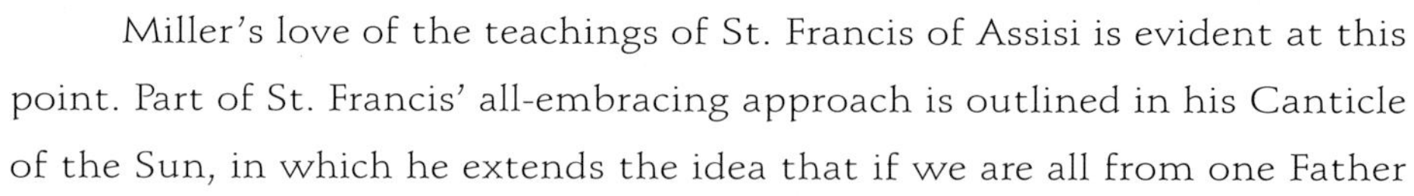

Canticle of St. Francis on Lelant Beach. Detail

Miller's love of the teachings of St. Francis of Assisi is evident at this point. Part of St. Francis' all-embracing approach is outlined in his Canticle of the Sun, in which he extends the idea that if we are all from one Father then we are all kin. To demonstrate that he personifies the elements, and many of the titles of the most recent works refer to Brother Sun and Sister Moon, and depict the dancing figure.

"What this canticle expresses is that St Francis saw the whole of creation as one thing, and not as something that is there for man's use. He praises all the elements, nature, creation, the sun and the moon, in turn," says Miller. "This is extraordinary when you think that it was very much an age when the Church was more concerned with its own power, and not with the notion that there is something more powerful than itself."

A seminal painting in the latest collection is "The Morning Beach". It is about crossing thresholds, about looking into the beyond with a sense of yearning, but unusually for Miller there are two figures rather than one. It is inspired by something quite specific.

Morning Beach. Detail

"The incident from the gospel of John is one that has exercised me because, like Lazarus, Peter was offered a second chance, having denied Jesus at the time of the trial and crucifixion," explains Miller. "He must have felt that everything in his life had fallen apart at that moment because he had denied the man who had become so important to him, who had changed his life completely and whom he had subsequently seen die. When the disciple John said, "It is the Master," one understands how Peter immediately leapt out of the boat and waded ashore. It is that moment that I have been trying to paint for so long and with this painting I think I have come as close as I can possibly come to it."

That moment. In essence it is about being human. About raising our eyes and looking at all we understand and don't understand, aching to reach but not reaching, to know but not knowing.

After his mother's death Miller wrote: "Standing back, I am still amazed at the response of so many people to the new work. It is as though the need to communicate to a single person at a deeper level has opened up lines of communication to so many more people that I could have imagined."

If you like, you can stand in front of a John Miller painting and just bask in the ever-present glow, lose yourself in the most glorious colours on canvas. You can resist all the other levels that are there and appreciate the work just as much. But the fact is that Miller doesn't shy away from the big questions in his art, the ones with no answers at all. And he manages to do this without being heavy, or getting complicated, but just by celebrating the moment. ■

Emma Burn and Michael Truscott
at Sancreed 1990

May Sunrise. Oil

Morning Sun. Oil

"Are they beach scenes of Tresco in the Scilly Isles, of Hayle sands near St Ives or far off Bermudan Islands - or does it really matter? They are somewhere special, perhaps a beach in your life, that childhood memory, or a space found in a busy schedule away from the noise and clamour of the modern day world, time perhaps to celebrate nature and one's own existence within it".

From the catalogue foreword for 1995 exhibition © David Messum

". . . there is a lyrical quality about his work, a sense of nature on the move, that is deeply satisfying."

© Frank Ruhrmund, "Western Morning News," 1973

September Horizon. Oil

Penwith Beach. Oil

May Horizon. Oil

Sunrise. Oil

"He has the gift of taking us away from this often arid world, and leading us to an awareness of our secret selves. We find ourselves unexpectedly awakened. We see on our wall a painting which has become our best friend."

From the catalogue foreword "Great Spaces in a Whisper".

Beach Figure with Orange Sun. Oil

Porth Kidney Horizon. Gouache

"As no one else in my experience, he succeeds in capturing the enchanting (in the proper sense of the word) and yet alien feeling of this Arthurian landscape."

© Max Wykes-Joyce,
"International Herald Tribune", 1975

"Recent watercolours of Cornwall, the Thames and Venice, . . . at The Brotherton Gallery, London, . . . show Miller to be adept at small watercolours that, for all their sense of mystery, are meticulously detailed."

© Max Wykes-Joyce,
"New York Times" & "Washington Post", 1981

"The early morning, when the light was a prayer and the first sun a song of promise, a burst of blazing colour he tried to catch as it hit the sea, making it anything, everything, but blue . . . During the years I have known Michael and John, they have shared with me a sense of integrity to a *place*, carving out an area of calm. I suspect that when his work is not going well it is mainly because he hopes always to capture something of that for others – and it's sometimes elusive."

From the catalogue foreword "John Miller".

The Morning Beach. Oil

"He can do nothing without grace, nothing without art, as this exhibition shows. As with writing, so with painting, the talent goes into the first draft. But the art, the discipline, the experience and the sheer professionalism go into the second, third and fourth, ad infinitum. No painter has a better right to Whistler's dictum that when you buy one of his pictures, you are paying for the experience of a lifetime. Make no mistake: Miller's paintings, like the calm face that smiles at you, are the reconciliation of a turbulent and uncompromising spirit, whose quest has been made a great deal harder by an ability to feel responsible for practically everything and every one around it."

From the catalogue foreword "New Horizons". © John le Carre, 1982

From a sketchbook

Pentle Bay, Isles of Scilly. Oil

Quiet Bay. Gouache

"The most interesting discovery - in the exhibition "The London Season" – is John Miller, sometime chairman of the Newlyn Society of Artists, who has a pearly way of presenting the Cornish landscape of a quite different kind from that normally portrayed. His works have something of the feeling of the symbolist paintings of Osbert and Schwabe . . . "

© Max Wykes-Joyce, "Arts Review", 1975

"I think of John Miller more as a Cornish Monet. No doubt he will laugh ... But he has Monet's absorption in rendering the exquisite surfaces of things ... in Nature. That is what John Miller catches for us in the endless variety of his exploration of its forms, and the colours of light."

From the catalogue foreword "Recent Paintings".
© A.L. Rowse, 1989

"Looking at them (John Miller's paintings) I am reminded of something Dame Edith Evans once said to me when describing the young Gladys Cooper: 'her beauty,' Edith said, 'was straight out of the bath.' John's paintings are likewise uncorrupted."

From the catalogue foreword "Reflections".
© Bryan Forbes, 1988

Penwith Dawn. Oil

Sunrise of Wonder. Oil

Red Interior. Gouache

Ultramarine over Violet. Oil

"At the time (thirty years ago) I singled out his "Lazarus" as being wondrous – and a particularly powerful and profound piece of work. I was not to know that it was to prove much more than a nine-day wonder but the start, as Celia says in "As You Like It", of something "wonderful, wonderful, and most wonderful, and yet again wonderful, and after that, out of all whooping!"

From the catalogue foreword "Paintings 1998". © Frank Ruhrmund

"These new paintings are a distillation of vision, they have a purity and power which is quite remarkable."

From the foreword "New Paintings". © Jean Shrimpton, 1996

Sun Rising over Bay. Oil

Summer Shoreline. Oil

"I watched him watch Venice and saw the results take place; his architect's brain analysing, his artist's eye assimilating. Surely to paint Venice one should be both. He allowed me to feel that my inadequate comments and pleasure in his work helped, while his calm wise counsel saved me from giving up my own work in despair."

From the catalogue foreword "Venice Revisited".

From a sketchbook of Venice. 1984

Three Figures on a Beach. Oil

"The answers to these pictures are no longer in the painter but in the beholder, and that's what good painting is about."

From the catalogue foreword "Interior Landscapes". © John le Carre, 1990

"But the message is clear: these are pictures which work on us, not by embodying an anecdote, but by going straight to our deeper instincts, which calls inevitably on going to the painter's also. In all abstractions there is bound to be, naked and unashamed, a species of telepathy between the artist and his public. Jung would have explained it in terms of the collective unconscious we all share. Hitchcock would have said that all consideration of the unconscious was hypothesis anyway – which never stopped him making heart-stopping use of it in his films."

From the catalogue foreword "Paintings from Two Decades". © John Russell Taylor, 1999

“For me landscape is the space I live in, whether it be countryside, seaside or a room. Every room has its own vistas and we each have our own interior landscapes.”

“I have found in Chinese and Japanese landscape paintings a powerful sense of timeless space. I have also found this in Turner’s watercolours and later paintings, some of the French Impressionists and the work of the American painter, Mark Rothko.”

“It is that timeless space I have striven for in my own work from the early bare trees through misty renderings of Venice and sunlit Mediterranean landscapes into this more recent collection of paintings.”

“Glimpses of the landscape through openings and gaps particularly excite me. The impact of a fleeting image in a car driving mirror can awaken me to the present and stays on until that visual surprise becomes a painting.”

“I moved to Cornwall from London in 1958 to celebrate a land I had already come to love. Now, I am joyful that, after forty years painting, those celebrations of Cornwall are in collections in many parts of the world.”

Photograph by Michael Truscott

3

2

1

6

△ Photograph by Phil Monkton

5

4

8

9

7

△ Photograph by Sue Danziel

1. With Father Max Mitzi O.F.M. and Brother Michael S.S.F. filming in Assisi 2. Donating proceeds of painting for Wheelchairs for Africa and funds for Breadline with Brother Michael and Toyah Willcox at the David Messum Gallery, London 3. With Marika Hanbury-Tenison in Istanbul 1975 4. A break from filming in Assisi 5. With John le Carré in Mykonos 1980 6. With Frank Ruhrmund in Saint Mary's Studio 7. With John Bartlett, Director of "A Painter in Search of Saint Francis" 1987 8. John's brother David on a visit to Cornwall 9. With Tim Hubbard on the terrace of the studio at Lelant

△ Photograph by David Cornwell

A Search for St. Francis

Artist John Miller leaves Assisi in his search for modern applications of Franciscan values. St. Francis of Assisi, who with his followers lived a life of dedication to the Gospels and to peace, was called "a very special Saint for modern man" by the Archbishop of Canterbury. The writer and narrator is John Miller, a lifelong follower of St. Francis.

Camera David Howarth / Film Editor David Taylor
Producer/Director John Bartlett / TSW Production
(from TV Times December 1988)

With Gary Rhodes at Sancreed for "Rhodes around Britain" 1994

The ceremony in April 1979 at which Lady St. Levan opened a collection of ten oil paintings depicting incidents in the history of St. Michael's Mount. The series was commissioned by Lord and Lady St. Levan in conjunction with The National Trust from John Miller, of Sancreed, the Cornish landscape painter. The paintings, an important addition to the existing, mainly eighteenth-century collection, are hung in the recently created picture gallery at St. Michael's Mount. Photographed (above) after the unveiling of a plaque are (l.-r.) The Dowager Lady St. Levan, Lord St. Levan, Mrs. Miller (the artist's mother), John Miller, Dr. A. L. Rowse (guest of honour) and Lady St. Levan.

With Sir Harry Secombe in the studio at Sancreed for "Highway" 1986

10. With the pupils of Stokeinteignhead Primary School below the studio in Lelant 11. A painting by one of the pupils © Matthew
12. In the Bahamas with Jane and David Cornwell (John le Carré)
13. Richard Demarco and Mary Stork with John at Sancreed House
14. Robert and Lucy Dorrien-Smith on a visit to Saint Mary's Studio

Public and Corporate Collections include:

Victoria & Albert Museum, London; Avon CC; Cornwall CC; Royal Devon & Exeter Hospital; Truro Cathedral "Cornubia – Land of the Saints"; St. Michael's Mount – ten historical paintings and a crucifix in the chapel; Law Courts, Truro; BUPA; The Burton Group; Cunard; Exeter Hospice; Sony Europe; John Lewis Partnership; Discipline Global Mobile; Groucho Club, London; Harlech Television; a collection of interior landscapes for Rhodes in the Square, Dolphin Square; River poster commissioned for "Art on the Underground"; Penlee House Gallery & Museum.

Crucifix for Saint Michael's Mount ▷

"Cornubia" Land of the Saints

Some paintings from the past

1

2

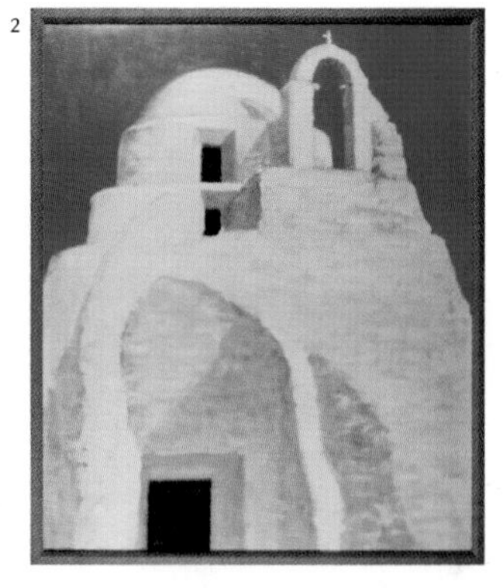

"John Miller's new painting, "Land of the Saints" which was unveiled by Prince Charles in Truro Cathedral earlier this week, confirms this artist's place among the great British painters. "It's a funny old life," said this quiet and contemplative man, whose paintings glow and irradiate light as though from some infinite source. "I am not a naturally talented painter, I have to work terribly hard." Above all this work has a remarkable dignity – worthy of its setting in this lovely Cathedral."

© James Mildren
"Western Morning News", 1980

3

4

5

1. Penwith Landscape 1973 2. Mykonos 1980 3. Sancreed Church 1973
4. Chiverton Farm 1987 5. Venice 1985

1

2

Saint Mary's Studio

3

△ Photograph by Brother Michael

4

5

6

7

8

9

1. Michael's workshop 2. The first lunch on John Makepeace's table. Dor Varcoe, Lady Mary Holborow, Heather, Geoffrey Holborow and Michael 3. John's workshop 4. Coffee in the studio, Dudley Sutton and Rose Hilton 5. Michael stretching a canvas 6. Rory McDermott, Boss, Jean Shrimpton, John, Michael and Thaddeus 7. Jean, Boss, John and Thaddeus 8. The John Makepeace table laid for lunch 9. Heather in her office

JOHN MILLER was born in London in 1931. Following National Service and a brief spell in the theatre, films and television he studied architecture and was articled to the church architects, Milner & Craze. He went to West Cornwall in the mid-fifties to measure the screen in St. Buryan Church for an exam and returned to live and paint there in 1958 with his lifelong friend, Michael Truscott, potter, photographer and conservationist. They travelled in a 1937 Austin Seven with twenty seven pounds between them. The journey took three days and at Sherborne a new back axle cost nine pounds. In 1961 he was elected to membership of the Newlyn Society of Artists and he became a Fellow of the Royal Society of Arts in 1964. He served as chairman of the Newlyn Society of Artists for a number of years during the sixties and seventies and planned the first modernisation of the Gallery in 1968. He was, at this time, consultant designer to the Hotels Division of the Rank Organisation.

John Miller
Paintings and Drawings

Michael Truscott
Pottery

Newlyn Art Gallery
11 - 27 October 1967
Lower Gallery

A solo exhibition in Penzance in 1974 brought his work before a wider public and he began to show in London, New York, Vancouver and countries in Europe.

In 1975 he held his first solo exhibition in London at the Anthony Fortescue Gallery and afterwards showed regularly at The Brotherton Gallery, Walton Street. He joined David Messum in 1982 and moved to the Portland Gallery in 2000. Other solo exhibitions with Frost & Reed, The Bath Festival Gallery, John Makepeace Workshops, The Grosvenor Gallery, Vancouver, Truro Cathedral, Camborne School of Mines, Penlee House Gallery & Museum and many mixed exhibitions.

He has made numerous broadcasts and TV appearances. 1981 "Made in the West" produced by Kevin Crooks for ITV. 1984 he played the part of Bramley in a TV film about the Newlyn School painters, "A Breath of Fresh Air" directed by Kevin Crooks. "Midweek" with Libby Purvis on BBC radio. "Highway" with Sir Harry Secombe, ITV. "Sparrow over London", BBC radio.

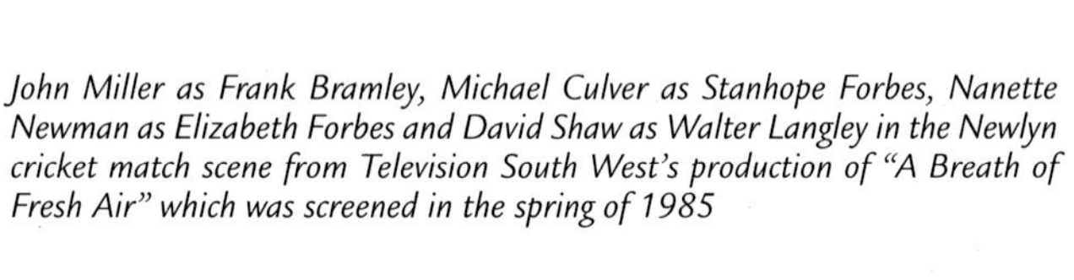

John Miller as Frank Bramley, Michael Culver as Stanhope Forbes, Nanette Newman as Elizabeth Forbes and David Shaw as Walter Langley in the Newlyn cricket match scene from Television South West's production of "A Breath of Fresh Air" which was screened in the spring of 1985

In 1987 he wrote and narrated a two part film for ITV, "A Painter in Search of St. Francis" directed by John Bartlett. "At home with John Miller" Tim Hubbard BBC Radio Cornwall. 1990 "Inspiration" Kaleidoscope, BBC Radio 4. 1991 Featured in "Dig", offbeat gardening programme on Channel 4. "Songs of Praise" BBC1. 1994 "Rhodes around Britain" with Gary Rhodes - chef. 1996 "Time of My Life" Dennis Cornish - Westcountry Television. 1999 "Collectors' Lot" - collectable West Country artists – Channel 4.

In 1992 he was invited by Robert and Lucy Dorrien-Smith to paint on the island of Tresco which led him into the Beach Paintings. After thirty one years living and painting in Sancreed, in the heart of the Penwith peninsula, he moved in 1995 to a Barn on Lelant Downs with a studio on the Hayle Estuary at Lelant. More recently, he and Michael Truscott have acquired a former Victorian church school in Penzance which they have converted into joint studios and a Silver Spirit Rolls Royce to replace the 1937 Austin Seven.

He is a Trustee of the Passmore Edwards Gallery, Newlyn and a Vice-President of Hospiscare, Exeter and Penlee House Gallery and Museum, Penzance. Member of Truro Cathedral Fabric Advisory Committee. Lay Canon of Truro Cathedral.

Books: "Cooking with Vegetables" with late Marika Hanbury-Tenison (1980), "Leave Tomorrow Behind" - autobiography (1989), "Sketchbook of Cornwall" (1991), "Seaside Sketchbook" (1993).

At 17 John Miller hung his work on the railings at Hyde Park

Triptych. Oil
(Hospiscare, Exeter
& District Hospice)
Photograph by
Mike Alsford

"I have concluded that, if I am to paint anything at all, it must be a celebration of all that is good and beautiful in this world."

Emma Burn is a freelance journalist specialising in the arts, whose articles have appeared in The Daily Telegraph, Arts Review, London Portrait Magazine and IDFX Magazine. She is also a chief copywriter for News Network, News International's digital publishing section.

Tim Hubbard has lived and worked in Cornwall for over twenty years. He has presented programmes for national and local BBC TV and radio, winning two prestigious Sony Gold awards. He has also written for national magazines, newspapers and Internet sites. A keen gardener of exotic plants, Tim Hubbard also collects the work of contemporary Cornish artists and is the author of "A Year in Cornwall with Tim Hubbard".

Chema Cruz is an art director, designer and illustrator. His work has been published in Mexico, USA and Spain. He now runs *mangoGraphics* in Penzance, where he lives with his wife and two children.

Simon Cook is a freelance photographer who lives and works in West Cornwall.